Tidal Waves

Sandra Woodcock

Published in association with The Basic Skills Agency

Hodder & Stoughton

A MEMBER OF THE HODDER HEADLINE GROUP

Acknowledgements
Cover: Dave Smith

Photos: pp 2, 14 © EPA/PA Photos; p 17 © Bettmann/Corbis; p 20 © Peter Ryan/Science Photo Library; p 24 Press Association/Topham

Artwork: Maureen Carter

Orders; please contact Bookpoint Ltd, 39 Milton Park, Abingdon, Oxon OX14 4TD. Telephone (44) 01235 400414, Fax: (44) 01235 400454. Lines are open from 9.00–6.00, Monday to Saturday, with a 24 hour message answering service. Email address: orders@bookpoint.co.uk

British Library Cataloguing in Publication Data
A catalogue record for this title is available from The British Library

ISBN 0 340 80063 1

First published 2001
Impression number   10 9 8 7 6 5 4 3 2 1
Year   2007 2006 2005 2004 2003 2002 2001

Typeset by SX Composing DTP, Rayleigh, Essex.
Printed in Great Britain for Hodder & Stoughton Educational, a division of Hodder Headline Plc, 338 Euston Road, London NW1 3BH by Redwood Books Ltd, Trowbridge, Wilts.

Contents

1   Tsunami

The sea is powerful.
Stand on a rocky shore
and watch big waves crash in.
See how high the waves can get
in a storm.
The power is scary.
Imagine a wave as high
as a ten-storey building.
Imagine its power.

Even a normal wave can cause terrible damage.
Imagine what a tsunami can do.

The most powerful waves of all
are giant waves
that can reach 30 metres high.
They wipe out villages
and kill thousands of people.
These waves strike suddenly,
with little warning.
Some move at over 800 km/h
– as fast as a jet.
They can cross an ocean
in less than a day.

Some people call them tidal waves
but we now know
they are not caused by tides.
In Japan they are called *Tsunami*.
It means harbour wave.
Tsu means 'harbour' and *nami* means 'wave'.
Tsunami is the word now used all over the world
It is the word for these huge killer waves.

2 What Causes Tsunamis?

Tsunamis are not like normal waves.
They are not caused by tides or the wind.
A tsunami is started by an earthquake
or by a volcano.
The movement of the earth
near to the coast or on the sea bed,
causes deep waves.
These waves are not just surface waves.
They go right down to the bottom of the sea.

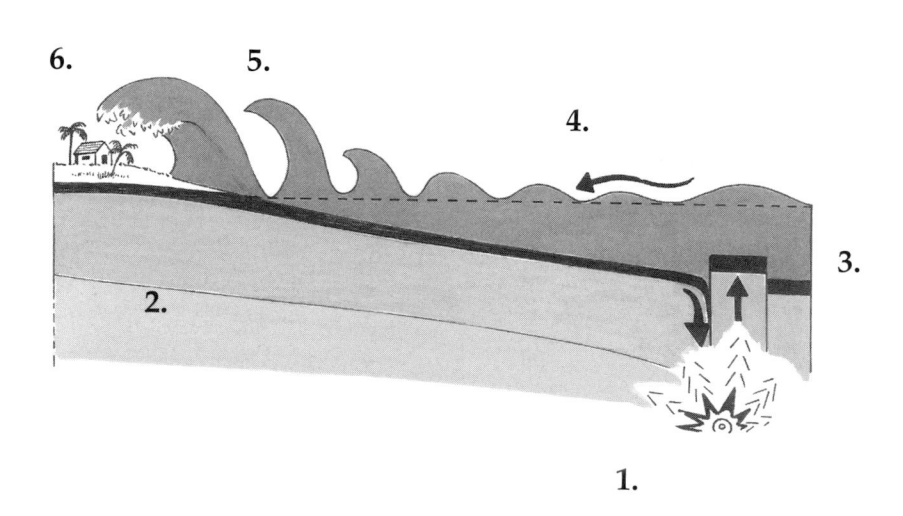

1. The earthquake starts under the sea only 18 miles from shore.

2. The seabed drops and water pours in.

3. The water is then pushed back up and forms a wave

4. This wave becomes higher and faster

5. As the tsunami gets near the land it slows down.

6. It crashes onto the shore with great force.

A tsunami can be started by an earthquake or volcano moving the seabed.

A tsunami that begins in deep water
does not seem dangerous at first.
It seems like a gentle rise and fall
in the sea.
The wave may be less than one metre high.
But the wave is very long (95 – 190 kilometres).
It also moves very fast.
As it gets close to the shore
it slows down, but it gets higher.
Many of these waves
are between six and fourteen metres high
when they crash on to the shore.
Some extreme waves are 30 metres high.

In 1896, a huge tsunami hit Japan.
It killed 28,000 people
and destroyed 270 kilometres of coastline.
Fishermen out at sea
had not noticed the wave
pass under their boat only minutes before.

3 Where are Tsunamis found?

Tsunamis can happen in any of the oceans
around the world.
However, most tsunamis happen
in the Pacific Ocean.
There is an area called the 'ring of fire' –
a chain of islands where
many volcanoes erupt.
This area has many problems.
Earthquakes under the sea
cause many tsunamis.

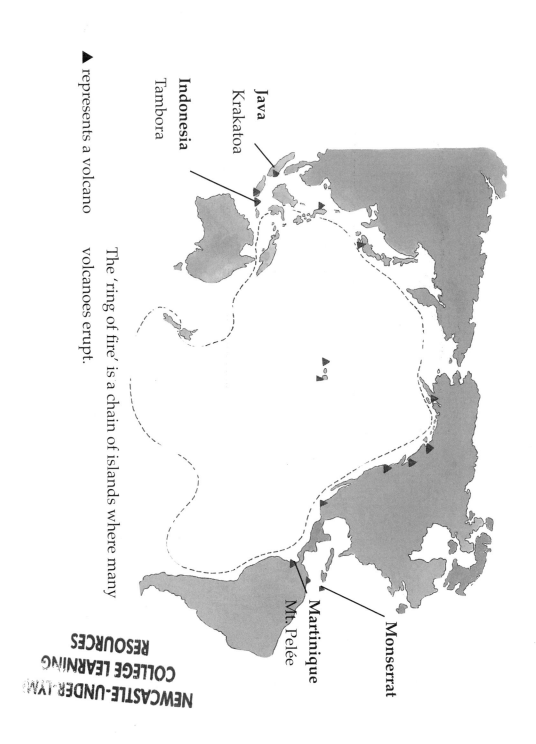

Java
Krakatoa

Indonesia
Tambora

▶ represents a volcano

The 'ring of fire' is a chain of islands where many volcanoes erupt.

Martinique
Mt. Pelée

Monserrat

A tsunami in the same place as the quake
is called a local tsunami.
But these waves can travel
thousands of kilometres to distant coasts.
Some of the most beautiful coasts
in the world are in the danger zone.
Many of these places are where
people go on holiday and
where surfers enjoy the waves.
They are places where people live and work.

The islands of Hawaii
have been hit by tsunamis.
Indonesia has seen 34 in the last century
and 150 have hit Japan.
California is also likely to see tsunamis.

4 The Power of Tsunamis

These giant waves have the power
to kill and destroy.

They can destroy buildings.
They can pick up ships like toys
and throw them onto the shore,
so they smash into pieces.
They can leave towns and villages
looking like war zones.

The death rate can be very high.
Most deaths are due to drowning.
But people are also at risk
from polluted water and damaged gas lines.

A tsunami can destroy a whole town. A tsunami hit this town in Indonesia in 2000.

Tsunamis don't all behave in the same way.
Some crash on to the shore.
Some move like giant walls of water.
Some just flood the land.
But all of them can carry rocks, trees
and buildings inland.

In 1883, Indonesia was hit by giant waves
as big as a 12-storey building.
Up to 30,000 people died.
The tsunami had started
when a volcano erupted.

Since 1945, tsunamis
have caused more deaths than earthquakes.

In 1946, killer waves in Alaska
caused much damage.
On one island,
a lighthouse stood 12 metres
above sea level.
It was five storeys high.
It was wiped out by a wave.
Tsunamis can carry their power
thousands of kilometres.
These waves from Alaska hit Hawaii,
almost 4,000 kilometres away.
They killed 159 people.

In the 1990s, there have been
many tsunamis in the Pacific area.
About 4,000 people have died.
People are often taken by surprise
and do not have a chance to get away.

A tsunami completely destroyed this town.

More and more people
are living and working
by the sea in the risky areas.
More and more tourists go on holiday
to these places.
Tsunamis may not happen often
but because they give little warning,
they can destroy on a large scale.

5   Tsunami Warning System

What can be done
to warn people who are at risk?
Tsunamis are difficult to predict.
Twenty-six countries in the Pacific
have joined The Tsunami Warning System.
The main bases are in Alaska and Hawaii.

Experts watch all earth movements
very closely.
If they think that a tsunami is likely
they can warn people who are at risk.
To do this they have to work out
how the waves will behave:
how fast they will travel,
how big they may be
and where they will go.
It isn't easy to get it right.
In deep water the killer waves
cannot be seen – even from the air.

Experts keep a close eye on all earth movements.

Sometimes a tsunami is predicted
but it turns out to be small
and does little damage.
The warning system
has led to many false alarms.
On 7 May 1986, Hawaii's main city,
Honolulu, was cleared of people
because of a tsunami alarm.
It was a false alarm
that cost the city millions of dollars.
But the warning system can save lives.

In 1993, there was an earthquake
in the Sea of Japan.
A small island was in danger
from a tsunami.
Just five minutes after the quake,
there were warnings on TV and radio.

Two hundred people had already died
before the warnings came.
But 1,600 people escaped
from a fishing village to higher ground.
They watched as their homes
were swept out to sea.

Japan has more tsunamis
than anywhere else.
In Japan they try to educate people at risk.
If people understand
the speed and power of killer waves,
they are more likely to follow advice.

6 What to do if a Tsunami is Coming

People need to know
the danger signs for themselves.
Just before a tsunami arrives
you may feel the ground shake,
you may see a drop in the sea level
and hear a roaring noise.

Low land near the coast is most at risk.
So the first advice
is to move to higher ground.
Some people don't want to do this
because it means leaving their homes.

People who are out on boats are better off staying out during tsunamis.

Some people think they will stay
to watch the tsunami.
They think they can run away
at the last minute.
But the tsunami can move
faster than people can run.
If you can see it coming
you are already too late to escape.

People who are out at sea on boats
are better off staying out.
The tsunami is most dangerous
when it reaches the shore.

It is a mistake to go back too quickly.
One wave may be followed by another.
It's better to wait for an all–clear signal
that it is safe to return.

Tsunamis have caused
many thousands of deaths.
They show the terrifying power
that lies in the natural world.
Even in the twenty-first century
there is little we can do in the face of
the nightmare of killer waves.
The best hope of saving lives
is to get people away in time.

How Much Do You Remember?

Quiz a partner to see if they know the answers or do the quiz yourself!

1   What is the name given
    to these killer waves?
2   What normally causes these waves?
3   Which country is most at risk?
4   Since 1945, what has caused more deaths:
    (a)   earthquakes?
    (b)   tsunamis?
5   What should you do if a
    tsunami warning is given?
6   Where are the main bases
    for the Tsunami Warning system?

Answers

1   Tsunami
2   An earthquake or a volcano
3   Japan
4   (b) – tsunami
5   Move to higher ground as quickly as possible
6   Alaska and Hawaii